YOU CAN DO THAT!

~ Duke Duquette

DUQUETTE BOOKS
Creswell, Oregon

Duquette Books - rev. 8/1/00
33433 Idyllwild Road
Creswell, Oregon 97426

For Carolyn -
for "being there,"
your energy,
your faith,
your love.

Luana anchored off Australia's uninhabited Direction Island
of the Cocos-Keeling group, in the Southern Indian Ocean
mid-way between Australia and India.
The beach palm records visiting sailors.

Contents

Also included within the text are 50 color photos
and descriptions from the voyage of Luana.

Introduction

In late 1991, someone in the office where I worked organized a contest. Everyone was asked to write down their dream; what he or she would do if they could do whatever they wished. Each person then turned in what they had written, but without their name on it. The contest was to see who did the best at guessing who had written each dream.

It was surprising to learn how little we really knew about the people we had worked with for so long. For example, one very conservative man--the type who might drive his car with windshield wipers going on a cloudy day, just in case--secretly wished he could be a high-stakes gambler at Monte Carlo.

Of the two dozen participants in the contest, four or five wished they could sail a boat on the ocean to far-away places. That was my wish too. But I thought how regrettable it was that none of us would likely ever in our lives do any of this.

I mentioned this to some of my clients, many of whom were retired people who did have the time and the money to do what they wished. They too thought that what I had realized was sad. They would love to have done those things they missed in life which age or physical limitation now made impractical for them. Their wishes now were more for things like their health, and their children doing well.

I was age 48. I imagined that if I was age 78 and God came to me and said something like: "Duke, what would you give if I turned you back to age 48 and you stopped what you were doing that you thought was so important at the time, and you took three years off and sailed on a sailboat to those far-away exotic countries? Would you give up half of what you have now, or more?" I think God would have persuaded me.

I went to my boss and told him that I wanted to take some time off and sail to different countries. He said, "OK, what do you need, a few months?" I replied, "About three years."

I owned a small sailboat which I sailed summers on a nearby lake, but that wouldn't work for what I had in mind now. All of the details--finding and properly outfitting a good blue-water sailing boat, learning where to go and when to go, knowing what to take along and how to sail on the ocean--were things that I then learned by reading and talking to knowledgeable people, while fundamentally believing, "I can do that." That does not mean that everything went perfectly, but I did what it took to get ready. I accomplished the adventure, and it came to be one of the grandest events of my life.

It was that same kind of certainty which had got me the job as a stockbroker almost eleven years earlier. I had an introduction to the branch manager but did not have the usually required college degree or investment experience. In the job interview I asked the manager if he would list his brokers in order of their production. After that, I asked if he would list them again, but this time in order of their ability. The two lists were not the same.

I told the manager that it didn't matter to me who those individuals were, I would do better than their average because I would do whatever it took to do that; and where I was short in experience or ability I would compensate with greater effort. I was certain that the average broker would not be working as hard as I was prepared to do, nor would they be as motivated as I was.

It was that same sense of belief which had brought me, at age 32 after watching runners in a footrace during a local festival, to resolve, "I can do that." I had no running experience and no regular exercise since high school where I was not an athlete. Regardless, if these people could do it, I could do it. I became a runner and went on not only to do it but to do it better than average for the next 23 years in over one hundred road races, two triathlons and eight full marathons including the Boston Marathon.

Motivation has always been a personal fascination. I have been a commission-only salesman for twenty six years. To deal with the ups and downs in direct sales, and to be positive at the beginning of each month when you have to start again at zero, takes ongoing motivation.

For more than thirty years I have read, collected and written motivational wisdom and have had a particular fascination with any achiever. In addition to an interest in people who do whatever they do with consistent excellence, or who are happy most of the time without needing an attributing reason, I see an achiever as being any person who has been able to lead themself to where they wanted to go. Not all of them were students of motivation. For many, a single thought or vision kept them focused and inspired.

Examples of that kind of inspiration can be:

*The greatest achievement was at
first and for a time a dream.*
~ James Allen

*How to get whatever you want:
Do whatever it takes.*
~ Unknown

*You prosper, or are happy,
to the extent that you
believe you deserve.*
~ Duke Duquette

When my sons left home and went on to college, I gave each of them a St. Christopher medal, on the back of which I had engraved the words "Yes I can." It has given me pleasure and pride watching them live with that attitude.

Only you know what moves you, and it changes as you are changed by your experiences. Things that seemed to be important can turn out to be not that important after all, while new visions or thinking may become very important, as that which influences you changes. While some thoughts will always inspire you, other thoughts will have special importance at particular times.

The following material is presented to you as a library from which you can draw personal inspiration as you need it, and to help you to believe that whatever your dream is, "I can do that."

*Behold your vision and
contemplate its reality, and
you will rise above all obstacles.*

~ Joseph Murphy
Your Infinite Power to be Rich

What Do __You__ Want?

If Success could be described as having what you want, and happiness described as wanting what you have, the common issue would be what it is that you want.

For happiness, what you want is less important than your ability to be happy without first needing something to attribute it to; to be happy as your natural state.

For success, you first have to determine what it is that you want to be successful at.

How to Find What You Want

The Truth Detector

Many people see their children or their spouse or their work as their identity and justification for existence. Who or what are you living for? Airline safety instruction tells parents to put air masks on themselves first. There is a reason. If you take care of yourself, you'll also be able to do better for others. You are the most important person in your life. If you are safe, strong, happy, you can be better for everybody. What do you want? What would you do if you knew that you could not fail? What particular part of that, or result of it, especially appeals to you? If you can imagine, you can find out what you truly want.

Lie detectors work because we react physically to thoughts. Because of this, you can learn what is true and important for you. First consider all interests, practical or not, and note your feelings about each. Don't hold back. Dare to imagine even the ridiculous, even that which you previously might not have allowed yourself to think about.

Then, no matter what it may be, if an idea causes you to smile or be excited; don't run off, enjoy it, look closely. Your subconscious won't deceive you. It deals only in truth, and it knows more about you than anyone--even you.

How to Get What You Want

Seeing is Believing

Most of us are seeing the same things. The difference between us is how we react to them. If you don't take control of your life, other people or events will control it for you.

Your subconscious directs your behavior to conform to the model which it has fashioned from its input. Truth, to your subconscious, is whatever you have exposed it to, and what it believes is what you get; wanted or not. It doesn't see good or bad; only what is. The more powerful, or vividly sensed an experience to you, the greater your retention and its influence upon you.

Remember in the movie *Gone With The Wind* when Scarlet O'Hara was at her lowest and vowed, "As God is my witness, I will never be hungry again." Once Scarlet established that, she did what it took to make it happen.

It is also apparent that once the subconscious has been set into an attitude, whether intentionally or by some experience, that it will continue to direct you in that way--as it did Scarlet O'Hara--unless it is stopped. That is why many successful people cannot quit, have room for little else in their lives, and tend to drive themselves into the ground.

This also partly explains why people who cannot seem to get anywhere may only see themselves in that light, why others who have achieved may never be satisfied, and why it is important for you to review your priorities from time to time and compare them with your feelings.

This gives you an idea how powerful a force your subconscious is. It is frightening to realize how one can be hurt or impacted for life by what it is that we take in. Yet this same human mechanism can act for your good when you are in control of it and know what it is that you want. It works equally well for good or for bad.

Until now, virtually all input to your subconscious has been by happenstance. You change this with visualizations and affirmations--new experiences for your subconscious. These change that which is you, and you behave--act and react--accordingly.

This is not done directly. With new beliefs your attitudes change, form your habits and direct your behavior. Your behavior is what produces the results you get. This is how you are the way you are.

In getting started, try to avoid thinking of whether something is possible for you. Just focus on what it may be that you want to do, or have, or how you would like to be. Then envision yourself very clearly there; seeing even small details, speaking as you would speak, doing what you would be doing, and seeing other people react positively as you confidently and happily conduct your life.

Try to bring as many of your senses into this experience as you can; especially your feelings. After you have made a decision and a beginning, and continued to nurture your vision, your subconscious will learn this reality and adjust your behavior to take you into your new situation. It is as though you've snapped in a new circuit board.

Let's say that you want to write classical music, and what is most exciting to you is the thought of hearing your work played by a symphony orchestra. Your affirmations might include: "I write beautiful music." "I love hearing the orchestra performing my music."

Your visualizations might include that of your being in a filled concert hall. Everyone becomes quiet. Then the music begins, and it is beautiful, beginning softly then building to a powerful ending followed by thundering applause. Look very closely. See every detail; the sounds, the faces, your happiness.

You see it, hear it, feel it. To your subconscious, it has occurred. All that remains then is for you to behave as "normal" and do what you do--compose. Sure, you'll have problems, like other composers do, but your subconscious will react accordingly and you will do what is necessary to solve them because you know the result--you were there.

So place your order. Tell your subconscious, with positive affirmations, who and how you are. Show it, with vivid visualizations, its new model for you. This mechanism is built into you and is there to serve you.

How to Get the Most
From the Material

Certain ones of the following thoughts, "Wisdom for Direction and Motivation," will have the most value to you at this point in your life. But read each one, and ask yourself "Is this the way I would like to think and behave?"

If your answer is a strong "yes." or even a "yes-yes," mark it with a Y or a Y-Y. If it doesn't feel like either of those, but might still be of value to you, mark it V. Otherwise leave it unmarked.

After you've done the earlier exercise and considered what you truly want, review the Y-Ys and pick your favorite four or five quotes. Write them onto small cards. Then memorize each; and as you do, visualize yourself using that in your life. Do that with as much detail and as vividly as you can. This will associate that thought with meaning for you, and begin its influence upon your personality.

Next, arrange the thoughts in order of their importance to you and place the cards where you'll see them both early and late in the day, such as on your nightstand or dressing mirror. Try to read each thought at least twice daily. While getting ready for your day, let your thinking come from these influences, and flow to any other positive thoughts.

Your day should enjoy a positive start that not only stays with you but keeps you aware of acting or reacting in the way that you would be. Before your day starts, perhaps on your way to work, do your affirmations and visualizations. This should further energize you. At the end of the day, review your cards again while reflecting on your days experiences. Consider how you were that day, how you might have been and still want to be different, the direction you want to be going in, and other positive thoughts that this may lead to. Lastly, for a better sleep and to give your subconscious something beneficial to do while you sleep, do your affirmations and visualizations.

As you become satisfied with your knowledge and acceptance of the thoughts on your cards, replace them with new ones and rearrange their priority. As these influences effect your thinking, your behavior should reflect your new wisdom and inspiration, empowering you to trust your feelings and to be the way you want to be.

Things change--but that's the idea; so the process of determining what you want to have or do, or how you want to be is not something which you can do once and for all. As you learn, you understandably change, and what you want can change. Meanwhile, the process itself can lead you to somewhere other than where you could have imagined, or imagined possible for you, before you started.

Wherever you are in your life, inspiration found within the following personal library of wisdom can always motivate and empower you.

*Wisdom for Direction
and Motivation*

The first ocean crossing. The energy of the boat.
Port rail awash as Luana leaves Cabo San Lucas, Baja, Mexico,
bound for Hilo, the "Big Island," Hawaii, three weeks away.

~~~~~~

The first law of personal leadership:
I am responsible
for what happens to me.
~ Duke Duquette

To get what you want,
first determine what it is,
and then what it costs.
Then pay that price.
~ Bunker Hunt

You'll never amount to anything, Einstein.
~ One of Einstein's elementary school teachers

~~~~~~

*What happens
is not nearly as important
as your reaction to it.*

~ Ed Foreman

*It is not your inspirations
or brilliant ideas so much as
your everyday thoughts
that control your life.*

~ *Science of Mind*

*They've got us surrounded again,
the poor bastards.*

~ Gen. Creighton V. Abrams

A "getaway" tropic island beckons to be explored, to lay in the sand and warm water and forget that you were going anywhere else in the first place. Part of Australia's Cocos-Keeling group in the southern Indian Ocean. The only inhabitants are chickens.

*Life is what's happening
when you're busy making plans.*

~ John Lennon

*God grant me:
The clarity to know what I want.
The inspiration to lead myself.
The nature to expect good.
The openness of childhood.*

~ Duke Duquette

*I couldn't wait for success...
so I went ahead without it.*

~ Jonathan Winters

Coral reef formations surround the San Blas Islands,
protecting them from large waves and providing much to see
underwater. This was Luana's first landfall after leaving Barbuda
in the eastern Caribbean. The two-masted boat, Tree of Life,
was beginning her circumnavigation westward from the
U.S. East Coast, while Luana was near completing hers.
Both vessels were bound next for the Panama Canal.

*Most people go after
what they believe they can get,
instead of what they want.*

~ Lyle Nelson

*You are never given a wish
without also being given
the power to make it come true.*

~ Richard Bach
Illusions

*The question is not so much
whether or not you are afraid,
but who is in control.*

~ Rev. Hal Milton

The Vavau Group in the northern Kingdom of Tonga islands,
1,200 miles below the equator in the South Pacific. A scene
much as it would have looked to the first explorers. Fiji,
Luana's next destination, lays 450 miles due west over the horizon.

*True charity is helping those
you have every reason to believe
would not help you.*

~ Unknown

*Confidence comes from conquering
fear of change.*

~ Dennis O'Grady
Taking Fear out of Changing

*If you don't have a dream,
if you don't have a dream,
how you 'gonna have a dream come true?*

~ "Happy Talk"
South Pacific

~~~~~~

If you have been hurt
and are unwilling to forgive,
you can never heal.

~ Rev. Ed Townley

You don't have to be sick to get better.

~ Joel Weldon

If you can't think of what to do,
do the next best thing.

~ Duke Duquette

Think slowly, act quickly.

~ Greek Proverb

~~~~~~

~~~~~~

You can only live happily ever after,
one day at a time.

~ Unknown

It's amazing how you're able
to turn problems into possibilities when you
eliminate the option of giving up.

~ Art Williams
All You Can Do is All You Can Do
but All You Can Do is Enough

Prosperity is never an amount of money;
it is a state of mind.

~ Louise L. Hay
You Can Heal Your Life

~~~~~~

Fanning Atoll, 1,000 miles south of Hawaii in the eastern end of the scattered Kiribati Island group. The sparsely inhabited coral ring is the remainder of a sunken volcano. Once the entry break in the ring is found there are shallows and coral heads inside, and absolute tranquility.

God grant me the serenity
to accept what I cannot change,
the courage to change what I can,
and the wisdom to know the difference.

~ Reinhold Niebuhr
Adopted by Alcoholics Anonymous

When you've learned the lesson,
the lesson will stop.

~ Duke Duquette

No kindness, no matter how small,
is ever wasted.

~ Aesop

Blue water, white sand, tropical sun, gentle ocean breezes.
The colors are real. Uninhabited Direction Island,
of Australia's Cocos-Keeling group
in the southern Indian Ocean.

*A bend in the road isn't the end of the road
unless you fail to make the turn.*

~ Unknown

*Until you make peace with who you are,
you'll never be content with what you have.*

~ Doris Mortman

*We all agree that your theory is crazy.
The question which divides us
is whether it is crazy enough.*

~ Neils Bohr
Physicist

Sunset under a "Palapa"--a shade overhang made from palm leaves--on a small, uninhabited island of a group 20 miles off of the Baja Peninsula, north of La Paz in the Mexican Sea of Cortes.

*When I race, my mind is filled
with questions:
"Who will finish second?"
"Who will finish third?"*

~ Said Aouta
Olympic gold medalist

*There can be a time when
the only way to win is not to play.*

~ Duke Duquette

*I shall become one of the greatest artists
the world has ever known.*

~ Leonardo da Vinci
Age 12

In the Pacific, off the California coast, out from San
Francisco Bay; Luana just sailed under the Golden
Gate Bridge and is south bound for San Diego,
the last that she will see of America
for the next three years.

You don't drown by falling in the water;
you drown by staying there.

~ Edwin Louis Cole

The person who takes no chances
generally has to take whatever is left
when others are through choosing.

~ Napoleon Hill
Think and Grow Rich

If you are miserable about all the things
you want and don't have,
think about all the things you don't want
and don't have.

~ Unknown

Dolphins like to swim along with the boat and play
under the moving bow, often coming in schools of
several hundred. Timor Sea, 150 miles off the
southern Indonesian coast, alert for pirates, bound for
the Australian Cocos-Keeling Islands.

*Every adversity carries with it
the seed of an equal or greater benefit.*

~ Unknown

*Yesterday is past.
I don't know what's going to happen
tomorrow, or the next day,
or the day after that,
but today I'm going to have a good day.*

~ Duke Duquette

*If you're going to be able to
look back on something and laugh about it,
you might as well laugh about it now.*

~ Marie Osmond

*Where there is no vision
the people perish.*
~ *Proverbs 29:18*

*A good plan implemented today is better
than a perfect plan implemented tomorrow.*
~ Gen. George Patton

*The determined find a way.
The less resolute find an excuse.*
~ Unknown

*The man of destiny knows it
before anyone else.*
~ Charles de Gaulle

*Both he who thinks he can
and he who thinks he cannot
are absolutely right.*

~ Henry Ford

The harder I try, the luckier I get.

~ Samuel Goldwyn

*Treat yourself at least as well
as anyone else you care about.*

~ Duke Duquette

It is very risky to play it safe.

~ Unknown

Sailing before light westerly trade winds. Downwind
from Antigua in the east Caribbean Sea to Panama in the west.
All sails flying, poled to starboard, and full.

*We are not human beings
having a spiritual experience,
we are spiritual beings
having a human experience.*

~ Chardin

*Have whatever feelings
you're going to have,
but do what you're going to do anyway.*

~ Rev. Hal Milton

*Sex appeal is 50% what you've got
and 50% what you think you've got.*

~ Sophia Loren

Mainsail reefed, sailing west in moderate southerly winds
crossing the Caribbean Sea east to west just out of remote
Barbuda where Princess Diana was having a getaway vacation
and paparazzi chartered planes were trying to spot her.

*The way to succeed is to
double your failure rate.*

~ Thomas J. Watson
Founder of IBM

*Forgiving doesn't mean
that it didn't happen.
It only means that
you will no longer bear it.*

~ Duke Duquette

*Most hockey players skate
to where the puck is.
I skate to where the puck is going to be.*

~ Wayne Gretzky

Cuna Indians densely populate a few of the larger San Blas Islands in the western Caribbean Sea off northern Panama. Thatched dwellings separated by narrow walkways cover virtually all available ground. On the chief's command, everyone canoes to the mainland and up river to tend the communal crops.

The hottest places in Hell
are reserved for those who
in time of great moral crisis
retained their neutrality.

~ Dante

Your future is not determined by your past,
it is determined by your ability
to think creatively in the present moment.

~ *Science of Mind*

When the student is ready
the teacher will appear.

~ Buddhist saying

This cave--on the north end of San Marcos Island,
Sea of Cortes--opens onto a small, hidden, open-sky,
inland beach. Entry is by swimming, or by dinghy
with head ducked. Off Santa Rosalia, Baja, Mexico.

~~~~~~~~~~~~~~~~~~~~~~~~~~~~~~~~~~~~~~~

If a thousand people say something foolish,
it's still foolish.

~ Unknown

If you would lift up your heart
to a higher level, you must first
paint a new life picture.
It may require the dying of what was,
for your rebirth into the new place.

~ Duke Duquette

It's what you learn
after you know it all that counts.

~ Unknown

~~~~~~~~~~~~~~~~~~~~~~~~~~~~~~~~~~~~~~~

A musician must make music,
an artist must paint,
a poet must write,
if he is to be ultimately at peace
with himself.

~ Abraham Maslow
Psychologist

If you haven't been fired once
before you're 30,
you haven't tried anything.

~ Tom Peters

Smile first. Ask questions later.

~ Unknown

Wind power steers the boat. The edge of the vertical
white "paddle", seen above the stern of the boat, is
set to face into the wind. If the wind changes or the
boat moves off course, the wind blows the broad side
of the paddle downward and gears and lines then steer
the boat back onto her course. It is fascinating to watch
the steering wheel turn with no one at the helm.
Solar panels help recharge the five large batteries.

The most important rule of time management:
Do the most important thing first.

~ Unknown

*From hurtful life experiences,
as with athletic training,
it is in the recovery
that we become stronger.*

~ Duke Duquette

*When you own who you really are,
you can lead yourself
anywhere you want to go.*

~ James Newton
Wings

Hilo, on the "Big Island" of Hawaii. It rains 150
inches per year in Hilo. This was Luana's first
landfall after the 3 1/2 week Pacific crossing from
Cabo San Lucas, Mexico.

~~~~~~

If it happens, it must be possible.

~ Unknown

I have been through some terrible things in my life, some of which actually happened.

~ Mark Twain

There is no greater waste of time than regret.

~ *Getting Things Done*

How to get whatever you want:
Do whatever it takes.

~ Unknown

~~~~~~

Seal Rock, in the Sea of Cortes Islands off La Paz,
Baja, Mexico. After anchoring, seal pups dart like
lightning around one's approaching dinghy. Visitors
have found the seals friendly enough to get in the
water and swim with them.

*Don't dismiss worthwhile advice just to show
that the giver isn't controlling you.*

~ Unknown

*Don't feel too bad
about an unwanted change.
It may be forcing you
to improve your situation.*

~ Duke Duquette

*A man must keep his mouth open a
long while before a roast pigeon flies into it.*

~ Thomas Lynch

A rocky coastal inlet in a protected bay on the
"Emerald Coast" of southwestern Turkey. Winds in
the Mediterranean are inconsistent in strength and
can come from any direction. Sailing boats
must often use their auxiliary motors.

*Only by attempting the absurd
can we achieve the impossible.*

~ Unknown

*The quality of a man's life
is in direct proportion
to his commitment to excellence,
regardless of his chosen field of endeavor.*

~ Vince Lombardi

*The essence of genius is
to know what to overlook.*

~ William James

Think twice; do once.

~ *Simple Truths*

Only the mediocre are always at their best.

~ Jean Giradoux

Those who are usually happy,
usually don't need
an excuse to be happy.

~ Duke Duquette

Whenever you find yourself
on the side of the majority,
it's time to stop and reflect.

~ Mark Twain

Eagles don't flock.

~ H. Ross Perot

*Am I not destroying my enemies
when I make them my friends?*

~ Abraham Lincoln

*Moments of our lives can be eternal,
without being everlasting.*

~ Harold Kushner

When the horse dies, get off.

~ Kinky Friedman

Balancing rock, near Pichilinque in southeast Baja, north of La Paz, Mexico. Not only is it remarkable to see such a mass balanced naturally on such a tiny neck, but to see that this phenomenon remains intact while adjacent to a public beach.

*There is no king who has not had a slave
among his ancestors, and no slave who
has not had a king among his.*
~ Helen Keller

*We can't go back later
and live lost experiences.
Are you missing the present
over preoccupation with the past,
the future, or, in perspective,
the unimportant?*
~ Duke Duquette

*The moment of victory is much too short
to live for that and nothing else.*
~ Martina Navratilova

A protected anchorage on Kaio Bay
in one of the southern fingers of the Greek
Peloponnese Peninsula in the mid-Mediterranean Sea.
Few visitors come to this part of Greece.
En route from Athens to Palermo, Sicily.

Unless each day can be looked back upon
by an individual as one in which
he has had some fun, some joy,
some real satisfaction, that day is a loss.

~ Dwight D. Eisenhower

There will come a time
when you believe everything is finished.
That will be the beginning.

~ Louis L'Amour

First you develop an idea
then it develops you.

~ Unknown

Every person, all the events of your life,
are there because you have drawn them there.
What you choose to do with them
is up to you.

~ Richard Bach
Illusions

If you do not dream, you limit your ideas.
Without ideas, you limit your planning.
Without plans, you will not reach.
Unless you reach, you cannot grasp.

~ Duke Duquette

If we agree on everything,
only one of us is necessary.

~ Dan Millman
Everyday Enlightenment

Myriad of palm-filled, reef-protected islands
resembling ships on the horizon. The all-powerful
Cuna Indian chief assigns and rotates one or two families
per island to live and to harvest and sell the coconuts.
In the western Caribbean sea.
San Blas Islands, northern Panama.

Periodically ask yourself,
"If it wasn't for X, I would be happy."
What are your fears about X?
Is the true, bottom line fear,
that of not being able to cope?
Is this really about
how you feel about yourself?
When you have overcome
the bottom line fear,
the others fade.

~ Duke Duquette

If you do what everybody else is doing,
the result will be the same
as everybody else's.

~ John Templeton

A mound of empty sea shells on shore in the Sea of
Cortes islands off Baja, Mexico. While most of the
islands are uninhabited and appear barren, the waters
are abundant with life. Hardy fishermen come here
from nearby Baja through choppy waters in small,
open outboard motor boats called *pangas*.

*Happiness begins on the inside
and flows out.
It doesn't exist on the outside and flow in.*

~ Dennis Wholey
Are You Happy?

*Ask, and it shall be given you;
seek, and ye shall find;
knock, and it shall be opened unto you.*

~ Matthew 7:7

*We are continually faced
by great opportunities brilliantly
disguised as insoluble problems.*

~ Andrew Matthews
Being Happy

*Stop cutting from time to time
and sharpen the saw.*

~ Stephen R. Covey
*The 7 Habits of
Highly Successful People*

*Before you will accept that
you can choose better than what
you have, you need to accept
that you chose where you are.*

~ Duke Duquette

*My house burned down,
but now I can see the moon.*

~ Japanese proverb

Dusk at a white beach near Pichilinque in southeast Baja,
north of La Paz, Mexico. A well-protected anchorage
means no rolling at anchor and no surf to cross
when coming ashore in the dinghy.

~~~~~~

When you lift yourself up
you lift up those around you.

~ Rev. Baine Palmer

We cannot move forward unless
we are willing to step out onto the bridge
and be vulnerable.

~ Rev. Ed Townley

When you give,
more than that comes back to you.

~ Duke Duquette

We will either find a way or make one.

~ Hannibal

~~~~~~

Cochin, on the Sea of Arabia coast of southwestern India.
Passenger ferries off Bolgaty Island at sunset in Cochin Harbor.
This was the first landfall after crossing the equator
into the northern hemisphere from the Indian Ocean
and the Cocos-Keeling Islands.

In Alice in Wonderland,
Alice asks the Cheshire Cat for directions:
"Would you tell me please,
which is the way to go from here?"
"That depends a good deal on where
you want to get to," says the cat.
"I don't much care where..." says Alice.
"Then it doesn't matter which way you go,"
says the cat.

~ Lewis Carroll

It is not because things are difficult
that we do not dare. It is because
we do not dare that things are difficult.

~ Seneca

*Imagination is more important
than knowledge.*

~ Einstein

You haven't failed until you've given up.

~ *Mark Haroldsen*

*If you want something done,
ask a busy person.*

~ Duke Duquette

*If the captain's highest priority
was the preservation of the ship,
he would never set out to sea.*

~ Unknown

The Blue Mosque of Istanbul, Turkey, near the
beginning of the Straits of Bosporus into the Black Sea.
Turkish sultans once ruled the known world from
Istanbul's Topkapi Palace. An obelisk pillar in the city,
called the millennium, is the point from which
all distances in the empire were measured.

~~~~~~

After eliminating the impossible,
whatever remains, however improbable,
must be the truth.

~ Arthur Conan Doyle
Sherlock Holmes

You don't learn nearly as much
from doing things right, as you do
from doing things wrong.

~ Duke Duquette

Find out what you don't do well,
then don't do it.

~ Unknown

~~~~~~

Sunset on the Niger River at Mopti, in Mali, western Africa.
The Niger has always been an important African thoroughfare.
Families live on small islands in the flood plain.
This was a stopover on an inland excursion into
the Sahara Desert to the outpost of Timbuktu.

If you want to launch big ships,
you have to go where the water is deep.

~ Conrad Hilton's mother

It is an equal failing to trust everyone,
and to trust no one.

~ 18th century English proverb

My biggest mistakes were in aiming low
and scoring a direct hit.

~ Lyle Nelson

It's never too late
to have a happy childhood.

~ Bumper sticker

*You can easily judge
the character of a man
by how he treats those
who can do nothing for him.*
~ James D. Miller

*As you can conceive of
and embrace your happiness,
it will come into your life.*
~ Duke Duquette

*You don't get a second chance
to make a first impression.*
~ Unknown

We shall never have any more time.
We have, and we have always had,
all the time that there is.

~ Arnold Bennett

The more you dwell
on what you don't want,
the more of it you create.

~ Louise L. Hay
You Can Heal Your Life

No matter what you do,
someone always knew you would.

~ Unknown

A rugged coastal anchorage on the Pacific Coast
of the Mexican mainland south of Puerto Vallarta.
Once frequented by smugglers, these rocky coves
now see only the occasional cruising sailboat, or
fishing boat coming out of the Pacific weather.

*Everyone has an invisible sign
hanging from his neck saying,
"Make me feel important!"
Never forget this message
when working with people.*

~ Mary Kay Ash

*No change = no difference.
To get to where you want to go,
you may have to leave where you are.*

~ Duke Duquette

You miss 100% of the shots you never take.

~ Wayne Gretzky

Falmouth Bay at Antigua Island on the western Caribbean Sea.
The First landfall after crossing the Atlantic from Gomera Bay
in the western Canary Islands, where Luana last weighed anchor
as Columbus did before his Atlantic crossing.

*The world in which you live
is not determined by outward circumstances
nearly so much as by the thoughts
which habitually occupy your mind.*

~ Norman Vincent Peale

Well done is better than well said.

~ Benjamin Franklin

*Don't be afraid to take a big step
if one is indicated.
You can't cross a chasm in two small jumps.*

~ David Lloyd George

In these Sea of Cortes islands, out from the Baja Peninsula,
are many places of total solitude, but for the occasional rifle
crack sound of a jumping ray hitting the water after springing
straight up from it. Barely visible thin strands of stinging
jellyfish mean swimming in a Lycra suit, but there is so
much to see in these waters teeming with sea life.

Management is doing things right.
Leadership is doing the right things.

~ James Newton
Wings

Happiness requires peace.
Peace requires--not necessarily forgiveness,
but: - Acceptance of the past.
- A change for the better.
- The passage of time.

~ Duke Duquette

Perspective; use it or lose it.

~ Richard Bach
Illusions

A mound of coconuts ready to be shelled and the white "meat" sold to Colombian traders by this island's resident Cuna Indian family. Small boys shinny up the palms and twist the coconuts until they fall. In the western Caribbean Sea. San Blas Islands, northern Panama.

~~~~~~

Even if you're on the right track,
you'll get run over if you just sit there.
~ Will Rogers

You cannot be anything
if you want to be everything.
~ Solomon Schechter

The price of greatness is responsibility.
~ Winston Churchill.

In each of us there are heroes;
speak to them and they will come forth.
~ Unknown

~~~~~~

Chacala Bay on the Mexican mainland between Puerto Vallarta
and Mazatlan in the Sea of Cortes. On the outskirts of tiny
Chacala village, in a wooded setting on this bay, is a small
but rustic and internationally known school that boards 10 or 12.
Visitors are taught Spanish, get to use it locally, and
enjoy the water, sun and solitude.

*Try not to become a person of success
but rather a person of value.*

~ Albert Einstein

Winners are prepared to be big losers.

~ Fran Tarkenton

*You may have to fight a battle
more than once to win it.*

~ Margaret Thatcher

*If you don't make waves,
you're not under way.*

~ Leonard P. Gollobin

The "Emerald Coast" along southwestern Turkey in the
eastern Mediterranean Sea is a haven of cruising sailors avoiding
the harbors and anchorages of western Turkey and the Greek Islands,
which are popular destinations of chartered boats. This is the
cliff-side village of Kekova, on a protected coastal bay.

Men who try to do something and fail
are infinitely better off
than those who try to
do nothing and succeed.

~ Lloyd James

If you want it, think it.
If you don't want it, don't think it.

~ Duke Duquette

Ships sail east, and ships sail west
on the very same winds that blow.
It's the set of the sail, and not the gale,
that determines where you go.

~ Unknown

Pago Pago (pronounced Pango Pango) Harbor at American Samoa in the southern Pacific, 950 miles below the equator. A protected anchorage for sailors, and location of Chicken of the Sea and Starkist Tuna plants. En route from Honolulu, Hawaii, to the Kingdom of Tonga.

The Chinese word for crisis
is composed of the two characters,
for danger and for opportunity.

~ Richard Nixon

I'm never a failure
until I begin blaming others.

~ Don James

For all things, there is a perfect time.
For every door that closes,
there is one that opens.

~ Unknown

Mauna Kea Bay, the "Big Island," Hawaii. This is an exception. There are very few places to anchor in Hawaii. In another bay close by, Hawaiian natives killed the explorer, Captain Cook.

*Genius: The ability to give
one's undistracted attention
to just one thing for five minutes.*

~ Unknown

Worry is the misuse of your imagination.

~ Ed Foreman

*If you can't fight or flee,
you have to negotiate.*

~ Duke Duquette

*If you tell the truth,
you don't have to have a great memory.*

~ Mark Twain

Remote Christmas Island (Australian), in the Indian Ocean.
En route from Darwin, Australia, to Cochin, India.
There was originally just the phosphate mine,
worked by a colony of imported Asians.
Now a busy resort and casino caters to wealthy
Indonesians able to gamble millions of dollars at a time.

If I keep a green bough in my heart,
the singing bird will come.

~ Chinese proverb

The secret of patience is to
find something else to do in the meantime.

~ Dell Puzzles & Games

People who deserve to be successful
will never take it for granted.

~ Unknown

There is a time for departure
even when there's no certain place to go.

~ Tennessee Williams

*Most of us believe in trying
to make other people happy
only if they can be happy in ways
of which we approve.*

~ Unknown

*You prosper,
or are happy,
to the extent that you
believe you deserve.*

~ Duke Duquette

*Pray to God,
but row toward shore.*

~ Unknown

*Never turn your back on a threatened
danger and try to run away from it.
If you do that, you will double the danger.
But if you meet it promptly
and without flinching,
you will reduce the danger by half.
Never run away from anything, never.*
~ Winston Churchill

*Things turn out best for the people who
make the best of the way things turn out.*
~ Art Linkletter

*Everything in moderation,
including moderation.*
~ Buddha

Dangerous approach to Pago Pago Harbor,
American Samoa, southern Pacific.
Hurricane season is November to May.
Ships having run aground are generally
not removable and are left to rust.

It's <u>all</u> good.

~ Bumper sticker

*People want to know how much you care,
before they care how much you know.*

~ James F. Hind

*The truth always comes back
to torment you,
until you accept it.*

~ Duke Duquette

*Please God, give me patience,
and give it to me now.*

~ Unknown

Villages have grown up around these massive ancient tombs
on the eastern Mediterranean Sea near Kekova Bay,
on the "Emerald Coast" of southwestern Turkey.
The tombs were emptied long ago.

Happiness is not what you get,
it's what you are.
If you're looking for happiness
in any thing, then you will always suffer
from a disease called "more."
All you will have known is striving.

~ Dennis Wholey
Are You Happy?

When you follow your heart,
doors will open that you
didn't know were there.

~ Joseph Campbell

When there is no wind, row.

~ Portuguese proverb

Kaio Bay. Southern tip of the Greek Peloponnese Peninsula.
Bunker type structures seen on the hilltops were family fortresses
in ancient war times. A few small villages and labyrinths
of stone fence ruins are all that remains of people
who once farmed these valleys.

Be big, think big, act big, dream big.
~ Conrad Hilton

Worry is about the future.
Regret is about the past.
If you dwell in either place
more than you do in the present,
your life is largely worry or regret.
~ Duke Duquette

If you ever take yourself too seriously,
take a look at your high school yearbook.
~ Unknown

An entire day was spent under these palms
on this remote, room-sized island, surrounded by reefs,
elaborate underwater coral formations, oversized starfish,
and exceptional snorkeling. In the western Caribbean Sea.
San Blas Islands, northern Panama.

*There is a difference
between striving for excellence
and striving for perfection.
The first is attainable,
gratifying and healthy.
The second is not.*

~ Getting Things Done

*The roots of violence are in the belief
that what's good for me is good for you.*

~ Unknown

*Unless you are willing
to start from where you are,
you won't start.*

~ Unknown

Houses cling to steep cliffs in the western Mediterranean Sea
along the Costa Del Sol (Sun Coast) of southeastern Spain.
Straight ahead, three days sail southwest along the same coast,
is Luana's next destination--Gibraltar.

Four primary rules in direct sales:
   1. Find a need and fill it.

   ~ Henry J. Kaiser

   *2. Your most important asset
      is conviction.*

   *3. Your customer is the person
      who can say yes.*

   4. Priorities:

      A. Talk to people.

      B. Everything else.

   ~ Duke Duquette

*If you don't have time to do it right,
when will you have time to do it over?*

~ Unknown

*Nothing in this world
can take the place of persistence.
Talent will not;
nothing is more common
than unsuccessful men with talent.
Genius will not;
unrewarded genius is almost a proverb.
Education will not;
the world is full of educated derelicts.
Persistence and determination alone
are omnipotent.*

~ Calvin Coolidge

*Live according to your highest light
and more light will be given.*

~ Peace Pilgrim

The picturesque Vavau Group in the northern Kingdom
of Tonga islands of the south Pacific has an abundance of
sheltered anchorages at beaches on beautiful island bays.
A popular stay of cruising sailors, especially from
New Zealand, 1,300 miles to the south-southwest.

*It doesn't matter what we do
until we accept ourselves.
Once we accept ourselves,
it doesn't matter what we do.*

~ Charly Heavenrich

*When nothing is right,
something is wrong.*

~ Duke Duquette

*If you ever get a second chance,
go all the way.*

~ Lance Armstrong
    1996 cancer patient.
    1999 winning cyclist, Tour de France.
    2000 winning cyclist, Tour de France.

Chacala Bay on the Mexican mainland in the Sea of Cortes.
A waiter on a surfboard from one of the thatched beach restaurants
swam out to Luana with a menu in his teeth in a Ziploc bag.
A shrimp dinner, served by the swimming waiter,
and the sunset were later enjoyed ashore.

Not asking for help when you need it,
is not allowing someone
the chance to be helpful.

~ Unknown

The man who views the world at 50
the same as he did at 20,
has wasted 30 years of his life.

~ Mohammed Ali

Destiny is not a matter of chance,
it is a matter of choice.

~ William Jennings Bryan

Falmouth Bay at Antigua Island on the western Caribbean Sea.
A steel drum band entertains evenings from an outdoor cafe high
on a hill overlooking the bay. A 135 mph hurricane blew down
many of the palm trees the previous year.

Most winners are just ex-losers
who got mad.

~ Unknown

Both the habitually happy
and the habitually unhappy
are seeing the same things,
but reacting differently.

~ Duke Duquette

If I had my life to live over again,
I'd make the same mistakes, only sooner.

~ Tallulah Bankhead

Caleta Partida--off the southeastern Baja Peninsula.
This bay between two islands is a popular protected anchorage
for cruising sailors and long-range tuna boats. Mexicans at
shoreline fish camps are happy to trade a fish for a can of food
or a used T-shirt, or the universal one dollar bill--
of which Luana carried a large supply.

Forget injuries, never forget kindness.
~ Confucius

We do not get rid of our faults
by calling attention to the faults of others.
~ Unknown

Success is never final.
Failure is never total.
~ Winston Churchill

The first law of holes:
When you're in one, stop digging.
~ Unknown

Clothing is optional, visitors are comfortable either way,
and these sheltered beaches are perfect for sunbathing.
Ispalmadore is one of the tiniest of the Balearic Islands, roughly
80 miles off the east coast of Spain in the western Mediterranean.
The only way here is by private boat.

There is no security on this earth;
there is only opportunity.

~ Gen. Douglas MacArthur

Success is how high you bounce
when you hit bottom.

~ Gen. George Patton

Personal leadership is acting
instead of reacting.

~ Duke Duquette

If it's not worth doing,
it's not worth doing well.

~ Unknown

To be wronged is nothing,
unless you continue to remember it.
~ Confucius

The essence of peace
is the acceptance of people
as they are.
~ Unknown

Prepare for the worst, expect the best,
and take what comes.
~ Robert E. Speer

These are the good old days.
~ Song title

Fall seven times, stand up eight.

~ Japanese proverb

Things do not change; we change.

~ Henry David Thoreau

*How you are
is more important
than who you are.*

~ Duke Duquette

*Insanity is doing the same thing
over and over again,
expecting different results.*

~ Unknown

Anchored at Friday Harbor in the San Juan Islands
near Seattle, Luana is newly commissioned, freshly
outfitted and completing her shakedown trial.
When fully provisioned she will be ready for sea.

You can't plant and harvest
at the same time.

~ Unknown

No one is inferior without his consent.

~ Eleanor Roosevelt

The enjoyment we derive from life
is inversely proportional
to how much we blame our circumstances.

~ Andrew Matthews
Being Happy

Normal is what you make it.

~ Unknown

Castle ruins above Kekova Bay on the Mediterranean
"Emerald Coast" of Turkey between Cyprus and Rhodes.
Ancient ruins abound in this part of the world,
which has been part of so many empires.

*Understanding isn't always necessary,
as long as you believe.*

~ Dean Koontz
Lightning

The discontented man finds no easy chair.
~ Benjamin Franklin

*Things happen so that you
will react to them.*

~ Duke Duquette

*If you're too busy to laugh,
you're too busy.*

~ Unknown

English Harbor at Antigua Island on the western Caribbean Sea. British Lord Nelson ruled the Caribbean from his garrison on this bay which is said to be one of the most beautiful in the world.

*The greatest achievement was at first
and for a time a dream.*

~ James Allen

Grow where you are planted.

~ Unknown

*Trust yourself.
You know more than you think you do.*

~ Benjamin Spock.

Always err on the side of boldness.

~ Patrick Buchanan

*No enemy is stronger
than one who does not know he is beaten.*
~ J. Middleton Murray

*If a trained flea
knew that it could jump high,
it would be free.*
~ Unknown

*Heroism is endurance
for one moment more.*
~ Norwegian proverb

Success requires no explanations.
~ Napoleon Hill

A scene like this was where Luana was conceived,
while staring outward with awe,
knowing that for thousands of years others also
had looked out over the intimidating-but-beckoning sea and asked:
What would it be like?
Could I do that?
Will I live my life and never know such an adventure?

Abraham Lincoln was great,
not because he once lived in a cabin,
but because he got out of it.

~ Unknown

Great successes are built
on frustrations, calamities, and failures;
not small successes.

~ Sumner F. Redstone

Begin with what you know;
you never know
where it will take you.

~ Paul Simon

*How silent the woods would be
if only the best birds sang.*

~ Unknown

*Then came the day
when the risk to stay in the bud was greater
than the risk to bloom.*

~ Wings

Glory is fleeting, but obscurity is forever.

~ Napoleon Bonaparte

*If you risk nothing,
then you risk everything.*

~ Geena Davis

Weighing anchor in Seattle and out from the Puget Sound
and the Straits of Juan De Fuca, southbound for warm waters.
There are oceans to cross, continents to find.
This is what Luana was built and fitted for--what she does best.
This is her element. She is at home.
The adventure begins.

First say to yourself what you would be,
then do what you have to do.

~ Epictetus

It can be done.

~ Plaque on desk of
President Ronald Reagan

If you don't take control of your life,
other people or events
will control it for you.

~ Duke Duquette

All glory comes from daring to begin.

~ Eugene F. Ware

Until one is committed, there is hesitancy.
Concerning all acts of initiative
there is one elementary truth:
that the moment one definitely commits oneself,
then Providence moves too.
All sorts of things occur to help one
that would otherwise never have occurred,
which no person would have believed
would have come their way.

Whatever you can do,
or dream you can do,
begin it.
Boldness has genius,
power and magic in it.
~ Goethe

Essentially

Things Learned

Daydreaming pays.

Opportunity is interruptive.

Expectation works.

Children see clearest.

Worries rarely materialize.

Inferiority is chosen.

Failure is productive.

Everything is optional.

Beliefs are knowledge.

Excellence is practical.

Faith is strength.

Attention enables memory.

Beauty is a decision.

Peace is acceptance.

Happiness is natural.

Success eliminates explanations.

Boldness is convincing.

No you can't.

Yes you can.

Worry abuses imagination.

Affirmations convince.

Acceptance overcomes agony.

Perfection is impractical.

Success is caused.

You decide your beliefs.

Focus enables genius.

Responsibility includes risk taking.

Choice is control.

Feelings indicate truth.

Conviction is power.

Blaming is counterproductive.

Luck is influenced.

Failure isn't total.

Success isn't final.

Impossible isn't absolute.

Maturity is ongoing.

There is enough time.

Opportunity is security.

Procrastination doesn't work.

Avoidance intensifies problems.

Bitterness kills.

Leaders fill needs.

Confrontation reduces threat.

Thoughts are things.

Destiny is chosen.

Asking is enlightening.

Regret is wasteful.

Problems disguise opportunities.

The worthwhile costs.

Friends care.

Character begets trust.

Persistence precedes luck.

Things change.

Successful relationship: 1+1= 3.

Faith delivers.

Purpose produces direction.

Moments last lifetimes.

Happiness originates inside.

Dreams reveal truth.

Accomplishment > achievement.

Excellence > perfection.

Important > urgent.

Persistence > talent.

Imagination > will power.

Tolerance > patience.

Conviction > knowledge.

Believing > understanding.

Relationships > activities.

Today > someday.

Mediocrity requires effort.

Followers relinquish control.

Courage requires commitment.

Responsibility is empowering.

Truth is freedom.

Vision defines destiny.

Change is natural.

Expectation reveals possibilities.

Passion compensates for disadvantage.

Givers receive.

You choose everything.

Boldness produces magic.

Safety has risks.

Vulnerability is strength.

No change = no difference.

Laughter heals.

Highest intelligence: Love.

Everything counts.

About Relationships

In a sustained and happy relationship:

Neither fun, sex, nor
a measure of love is enough.
That which you have together
should now or eventually total more
than what each of you has brought.
One plus one should equal three.
Your relationship should bring out
the best in each of you.
You should not rely on the other person
to make you happy. Each of you should love,
want, need, respect and be proud of the other,
and have the willingness, ability
and desire to give--and to receive.
Where these things exist, you should each have
feelings of certainty, joy, and gratitude.

*There is no hope of joy
except in human relations.*
~ Antione de Saint-Exupery

About Misfortune

It is probable and natural that unexpected,
painful events will take place in your life,
without your having done something wrong.
But we have the habit of looking for blame,
just as we look for reasons for good that comes
into our lives: "I must be doing something right
to deserve this"; not readily accepting that we
are worthy and deserving of such good.

In hindsight, you may feel that you could have
acted differently and prevented the misfortune.
In truth, do you deserve to bear that agony?
There is no "plan" to what comes into our lives,
but there can be reasons. Try not to agonize over
or seek a purpose to all misfortune--except
perhaps what there may be that you should
see in it, or gain from it, or do about it.

Bad things can and do happen to good people.
You are still good.

You need peace for happiness,
wisdom for peace,
perspective for wisdom,
and disappointment for perspective.
~ Duke Duquette

Success

What We Accomplish

- Having what you want.
- Has to do with what you have, do, or become.
- Too often deceptively rated by money.
- Success requires knowledge.

Objectives:

To discover, then to have that which is truly most worthwhile to you. This requires an honest evaluation, a decision, and a commitment.

You determine what you want, you establish what it costs, and you pay that price.

To want as you feel.

Success does not assure happiness.

Success is caused,
usually after the desire to succeed
has become greater
than the fear of failing.
~ Duke Duquette

Happiness

How We Are

- Wanting what you have.
- Has to do with how you feel.
- Too often deceptively rated by fun.
- Happiness requires feeling.

Objectives:

To live in the present, to trust, to see good, to expect good. Smile first. Ask questions later.

To be happy without a reason; such as having fun, or receiving good news. To have a child's openness, a wonderment, a readiness to laugh and play.

To feel as you want.

Happiness does not assure success.

Happiness has less to do
with what you can acquire
than it does with
what you can get rid of.
~ Duke Duquette

Goals are essential,
not so much for what they get for you,
but for what they do for you.
~ Duke Duquette

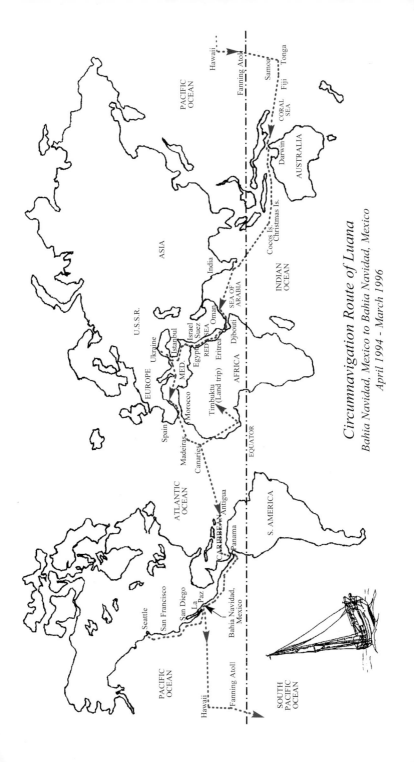

Circumnavigation Route of Luana
Bahia Navidad, Mexico to Bahia Navidad, Mexico
April 1994 - March 1996